We Pray, Pray, Pray
with Hanna, Grandma, and Caleb:
BE THANKFUL: Pray At Mealtime

Written by: Carline Constant and Gregory Constant
Illustrated by: Leena Shariq

Subtitle: Pray At Mealtime.

Text Copyright © 2024 by Carline Constant and Gregory Constant
Illustrations Copyright © 2024 by Leena Shariq
A Sprinkle Joy Publishing Book

For information contact us online at: www.sprinklejoybooks.com

Summary:
BE THANKFUL: Pray At Mealtime takes us on a spiritual journey with Caleb and his family. Grandma encourages her grandchildren to be thankful and develop valuable praying habits in all circumstances. Find out what happens when Caleb is eager during dinner time and can't wait to eat with everyone else. Will Caleb remember to pray for what he's thankful for before mealtime?

Subjects:
CYAC:: 1. Prayer Children's Christian Gratitude Realistic Fiction Book. 2. Faith Thanksgiving Books Children's Religious Christianity Realistic Fiction Book. 3. Godly Morals & Values-Prayerbook Gratitude Book. 4. Kids Giving Thanks To God-Picture Book. 5. Kids Spiritual Life Lessons-Christianity. 6. Raising Spiritual Kids-Praying Habits-Christian Picture Book. 7. Grateful Kids-Grandparent Christian Message Book. 8. Pray With Hanna Grandma & Caleb Christian Series-With Christian- Activities. 9. Christian Message Picture Book. 10. African American Christian Family-Realistic Fiction.

Identifiers:
Paperback ISBN # 979-8-9897681-2-7
Hardcover ISBN # 979-8-9897681-3-4
ebook ISBN # 979-8-9897681-2-7

Library of Congress Control Number: 2024904638

All scripture quotations marked (GNT) are from the Good News Bible Translation in Today's English Version-Copyright © 1993 by American Bible Society. Used by permission.

Printed in the United States of America
LCCN Imprint: Sprinkle Joy Publishing, New York.

10 9 8 7 6 5 4 3 2 1
First Edition: February 2024

Semi Realistic Art Style
For Ages 5-12

Sprinkle Joy Publishing Books

 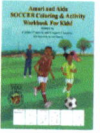 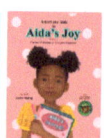    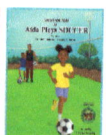  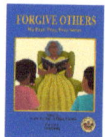 

www.sprinklejoybooks.com

THIS BOOK
BELONGS TO:

_____

WITH GRATEFUL HEARTS TO GOD!
To God be the glory!

****

This book is dedicated to my three sons, Gregory, Anthony, and Andy.

May God continue to mold and shape the three of you into responsible men.

Thanks to my family and friends for your words of encouragement.

Thanks to the editors for your contributions.

To all children and families worldwide.

-Carline Constant

Thanks to God for the many blessings.

-Gregory Constant

We Pray, Pray, Pray
with Hanna, Grandma, and Caleb:
BE THANKFUL

Pray At Mealtime

Written by
Carline Constant and **Gregory Constant**

Sprinkle Joy
Publishing

Sundays with my family always make me so excited. In the mornings we sing in church, pray together, and Grandma blesses our home.

GRATEFUL
Thankful
BLESSED

Later, delicious meals of all kinds of my favorite foods surround our table waiting for me to eat. Bright juicy oranges, tender greens, spicy browns, sweet melons, and tasty reds. *Yum!*

Bakes, smoothies, teas, coffee beans, spices, herbs, garlics, and onions fill up our entire house. *Gosh, it smells so good!* Daddy's music ring trumpets throughout.

Side by side with Grandma, my sister Hanna and I make homemade apple pie. We sprinkle cinnamon, sugar, and mix in butter. Grandma guides us as we gently take turns rolling out the dough while adding a little bit of water.

As our fingers shape the pie's edges, we laugh realizing some of the dough is on our faces.

"Grandma has a secret recipe in the apple pie filing, 'nutmeg'," Hanna whispers to me.

"Is that why it's always so yummy Hanna!"

She smiles so wide.

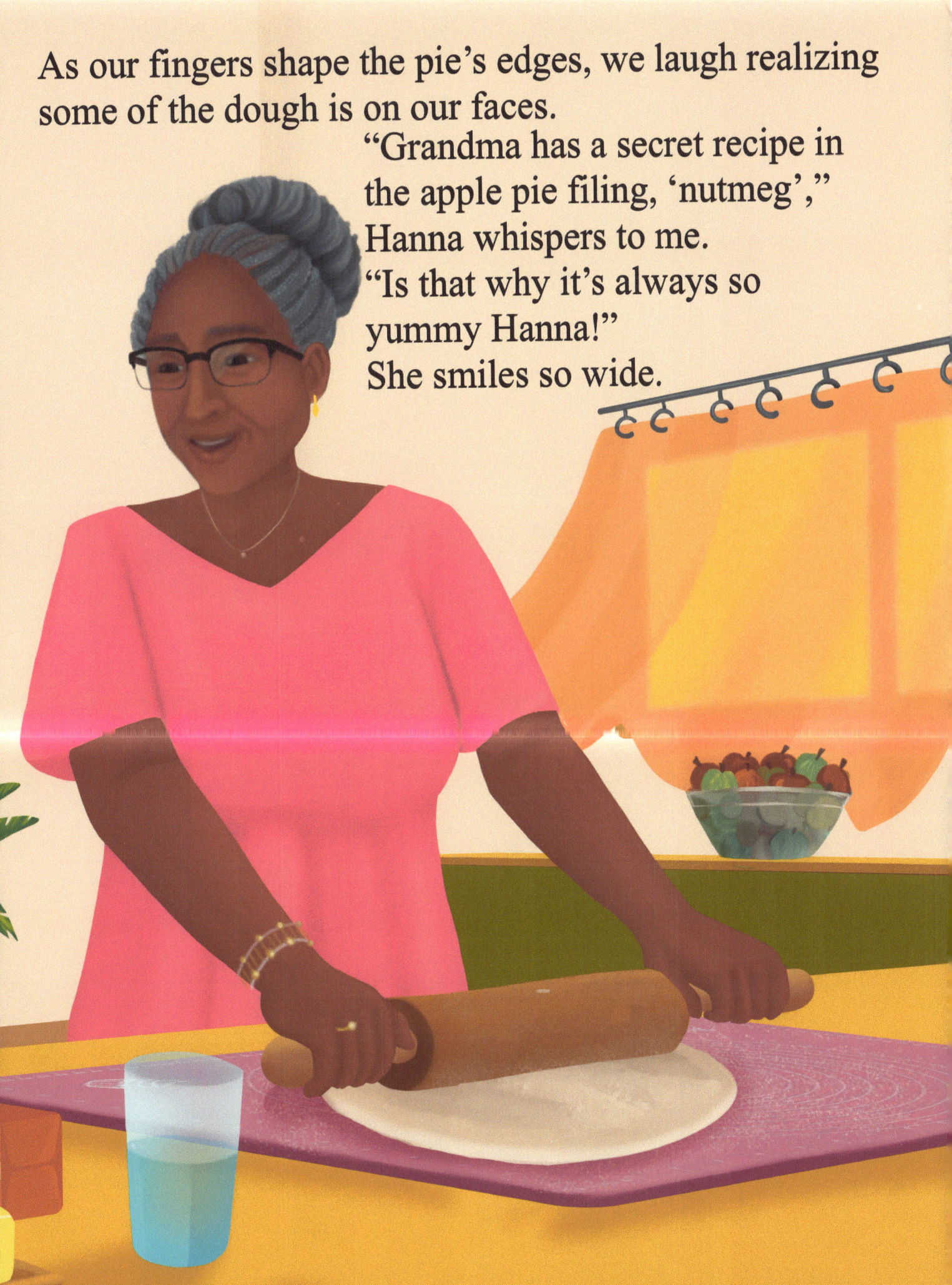

The smell of apples baking is almost more than I can bear. *I can't wait to eat! Maybe I can take just one taste!* When I peek in the kitchen to check on our apple pie, Mommy glances at me and says, "Caleb, time for you and your sister to set the table."

At once, Hanna and I wash our hands, fix the plates folding napkins tidily on each, placing the utensils neatly. "All set!" I report to Mommy as she places roasted turkey on a platter, with vegetables that surrounds it in the middle of our table.

My eyes follow Daddy as he walks over to turn off the blasting speakers, and I know it's time for our family to sit down together at the table. *Yes! Finally!* My mouth waters, I can hear my stomach growling.

The moment we take our seats, I can't help myself. I lean over, quickly stretch out my hand, take a piece of pie crust and place it in my mouth. *Delicious, hot sweet cinnamon and butter melt in my mouth! It's so good! I want more!* Eagerly, I reach for a turkey leg.

"Sweetie, not *YET*." I hear Mommy say.
"But it all smells so good making me so hungry."
"Caleb, show respect and mind your manners," Mommy tells me.
"Remember, we must say a prayer, first."

Grace

Bless us, O Lord, and these Thy gifts, which we are about to receive from Thy bounty, through Christ our Lord. Amen.

Grandma adds, "Yes, we must be mindful of who provides us with *ALL* the gifts on this beautiful table. Without mercy and love, we would not be here together."
Her eyes light up at the cross fixed on the wall.
My eyes also look up, before I bow my head.

Grandma told us to praise God always. I didn't express love to God and my family who spent time cooking for us. Oh, I must pray and be thankful for ALL that God has given me.

"Caleb, what is the first thing we must do when we sit to eat at the dinner table?" Grandma asks. "We must pray to God and be thankful." I look at my family and say, "I'm sorry for not saying thank you and for thinking only of myself."

Grace

Bless us, O Lord, and these Thy gifts, which we are about to receive from Thy bounty, through Christ our Lord. Amen.

I smile back when I see the warm smiles that break out on the faces around me. "Let us go around the table and say what we are thankful for."

Grandma begins. "God, as always, we give you thanks for everything. The Bible says, be joyful, always pray, be thankful in all circumstances." "God, I'm thankful for the lasagna that Daddy made for us, it smells so good!" says Hanna.

"Bless the gifts which we are about to receive Father God and we thank you for providing our family with what we need," Daddy says. "Yes, God, it's a blessing that we're here to eat together."

"For your love God, and all the hands that prepared the food, we thank you," Mommy continues. After listening to joyful words that flow around our dinner table, I say, "God, you give us so many wonderful things, I thank you so much." I smile at Grandma and Mommy.

Finally, we are ready to eat dinner!
Before I dive in, I close my eyes and say in
my heart, *it's a good thing to be thankful!*

God, thank you for your joy and all your many blessings.

✝ Bible Verses:

"Be joyful always, pray at all times, be thankful in all circumstances."
(1 Thessalonians 5:16-18 GNT)

"Always give thanks for everything to God the Father."
(Ephesians 5:20 GNT)

"I thank you, Lord, with all my heart."
(Psalm 138:1 GNT)

"Give thanks to the Lord, because he is good, and his love is eternal."
(Psalms 118:1 GNT)

Name: _____

Directions: Read and color in the Bible verse below.
Next, write to complete the sentence in the box.

Give thanks to the Lord.

Psalm 136:1

I thank You God for _____
because _____

IN THE BOX, WRITE YOUR OWN MEALTIME PRAYER,

Dear God, I give thanks…_____

_____

_____

_____

SEQUENCE OF EVENTS

HOW TO MAKE _____

Directions: Write the sequence of events or steps to create a meal. Remember to add the title of the meal.

Example: How to make apple pie.

Draw a picture:	**First** _____
	_____
	_____
	_____

Draw a picture:	**Next** _____
	_____
	_____
	_____

Draw a picture:	**Last** _____
	_____
	_____
	_____

BE THANKFUL WORD SEARCH

Directions: Find and circle the following hidden words.

BLESSINGS	BIBLE	FAITH
GOD	HOPE	HUMBLE
PRAYER	THANKFUL	

A	I	L	J	T	T	V	X	Z	B	J	A	Y	L	M
J	Z	Z	Q	F	J	H	P	C	F	D	D	W	G	P
E	M	W	H	G	T	H	A	O	M	S	G	V	A	R
Z	N	B	R	R	D	A	E	N	R	E	K	N	V	B
I	F	G	N	E	F	W	Y	P	K	E	C	S	C	X
U	J	H	D	Q	Y	P	A	W	H	F	K	G	J	S
R	T	S	O	U	O	A	A	F	T	B	U	H	U	M
K	M	A	G	P	N	W	R	Q	U	I	R	L	V	W
N	A	F	B	Y	E	E	A	P	K	O	P	I	K	L
H	D	C	P	L	B	D	H	T	I	A	F	H	N	T
K	Q	T	F	R	H	F	B	K	P	G	U	E	C	U
E	S	J	C	I	F	W	C	I	Q	M	N	K	T	T
M	G	A	V	H	K	E	M	C	B	Y	N	E	C	H
L	W	D	N	C	Q	G	F	L	A	C	V	U	T	S
E	L	B	I	B	B	L	E	S	S	I	N	G	S	B

WE ARE THANKFUL CROSSWORD PUZZLE

Directions: Complete the crossword puzzle below using the following words across or down.

~~Blessings~~   Bible   faith   God   hope
thankful   prayer   humble

Across

2. A _____ is a religious text or scripture that are sacred.

3. We are _____ by expressing gratitude or appreciation.

6. We communicate with God in _____.

7. _____ is our Heavenly Father, creator of people and things.

Down

1. When you have_____, you trust God even when circumstances are difficult.

2. To have **blessings** is to have favor and protection from God.

4. Respect of self and others is to be _____ .

5. Believing that what God says, he will do is to have _____.

 # WORDS TO KNOW

Blessings	Favor and protection from God.
Bible	Religious texts or scriptures that are sacred.
Faith	Believing that what God says, He will do.
God	Heavenly Father, creator of people and things.
Hope	Trusting God even when circumstances are difficult.
Humble	Respect of self and others.
Prayer	Communication with God.
Thankful	Expressing gratitude or appreciation.

About the Authors:

Carline Constant and Gregory Constant are a mother and son duo dedicated to spreading positivity through literature. They hope Sprinkle Joy Publishing books touch the hearts and minds of people everywhere. Each sentence, illustration and story telling idea of Sprinkle Joy Publishing books are made with love!

Carline Constant is a mother, author, and educator. She earned a Master's Degree in Education from Brooklyn College City University of New York.

Gregory Constant is an author, entrepreneur, and technology professional. He earned a Bachelor's Degree in Informatics from the State University of New York at Albany.

For information about Sprinkle Joy Publishing Books contact us online at:
www.sprinklejoybooks.com

About the Illustrator:

Leena Shariq is a self-taught, Pakistan-based children's book Illustrator and Portrait Artist. Always encouraged by her parents, Leena started freelancing at the age of 16, and now, after only four years, she has illustrated many children's books, one after another.
Her body of work consists of semi realistic illustrations and stylised portraiture.

(We Pray With Hanna, Grandma, & Caleb Series)
I AM THANKFUL
FORGIVE OTHERS
BE THANKFUL: Pray at Mealtime
Hanna's Blessings
GOD IS LOVE Coloring and Activity Workbook

Also, by Sprinkle Joy Publishing Books
(Aida and Amari Series):
The Champ
Amari and Aida SOCCER Coloring and Activity Workbook for Kids!
Aida's Joy
Aida's First Day of School.
Amari Plays Basketball.
Amari and Aida in HOW TO PLAY BASKETBALL.
Aida Plays SOCCER. (coming soon)
Amari's Helping Hands (coming soon)
Amari and Aida in FUN TIME Coloring & Activity WORKBOOK For Kids!
Thanks to God for ALL!

Thank you for your purchase!
Please leave an honest review. We read every review and they help new readers discover our books.

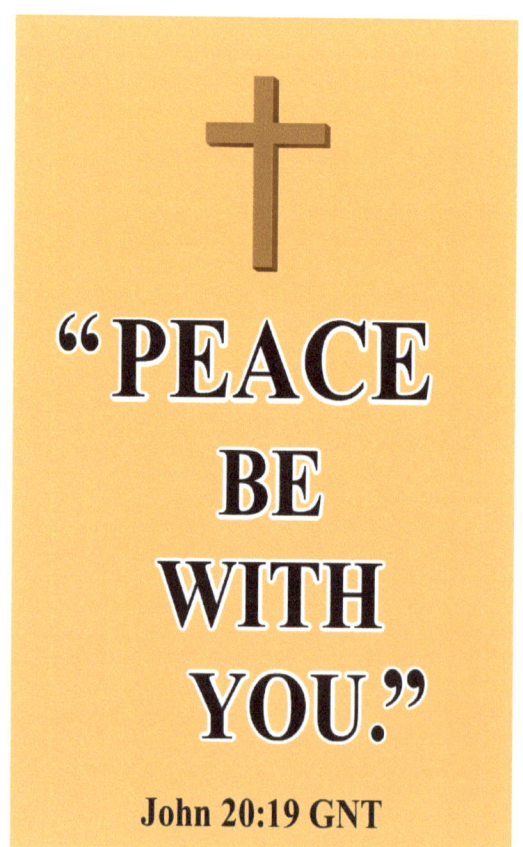

"PEACE BE WITH YOU."

John 20:19 GNT